A PUSH OR A PULL

THE DEFINITION OF FORCE

Physics Book Grade 5
Children's Physics Books

In physics, a "force" happens when two objects interact. What kinds of forces are there, and what happens to the objects? Let's find out!

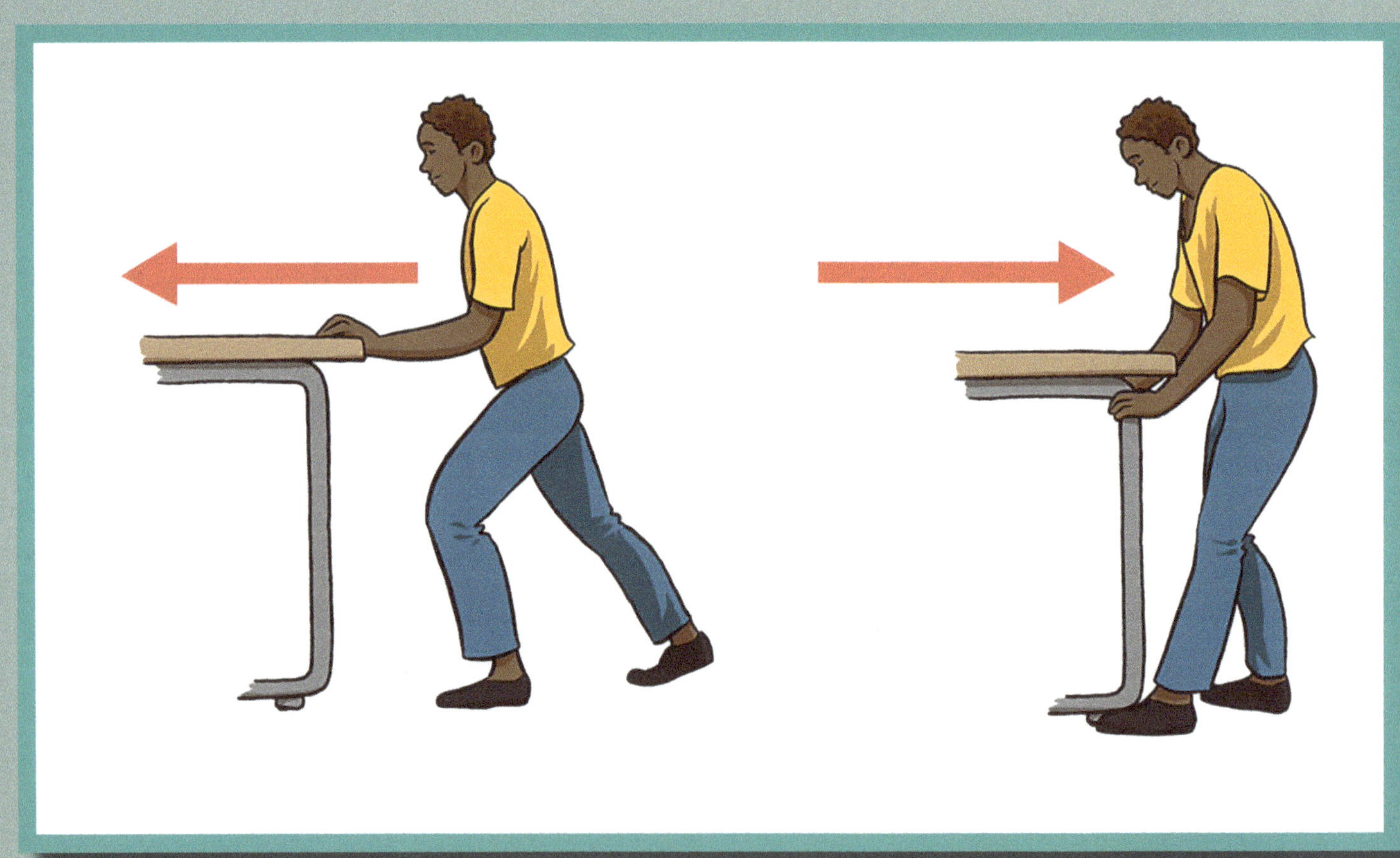

A MAN PUSHING AND PULLING A TABLE

WHAT IS FORCE?

A "force" is when an object experiences a push or a pull caused by another object, or several objects. Each of the objects involved experiences a force, and when the interaction ends, the force ends. In physics, "force" requires an interaction.

NINE: FORCES OF TWO TYPES

There are many different types of forces when objects interact, some when the objects are in contact with each other and some involving objects that can be far away from each other. And, of course, the same object can be experiencing many different forces all at the same time!

AN ACT OF SIMPLE WRITING INVOLVES FORCE

WHEN A HOCKEY PLAYER PUSHES OFF WITH HIS BACK LEG, A FORCE F IS EXERTED ON THE SKATE BY THE ICE.

OBJECTS IN CONTACT

Here are six forces that can happen when two or more objects are in contact. Each of them creates a push or a pull on the objects involved:

- Normal Force
- Applied Force
- Frictional Force
- Tension Force
- Spring Force
- Resistance Force

The Unsplash Book
The Unsplash Book

NORMAL FORCE

Normal force is the physics term for what is happening when two objects are in contact. For instance, you put a book down on a table. The book exerts downward force on the table and the table exerts the same force upward on the book, but from the outside, it looks like the book and the table aren't actually "doing" anything.

Applied force describes what happens when force is added to an object by another object.

The photo on the right page shows an applied force acting upon the object. The applied force is the force exerted on the toy by the young girl.

he could hear him, and faded and was gone.
375
391
held an open B
407

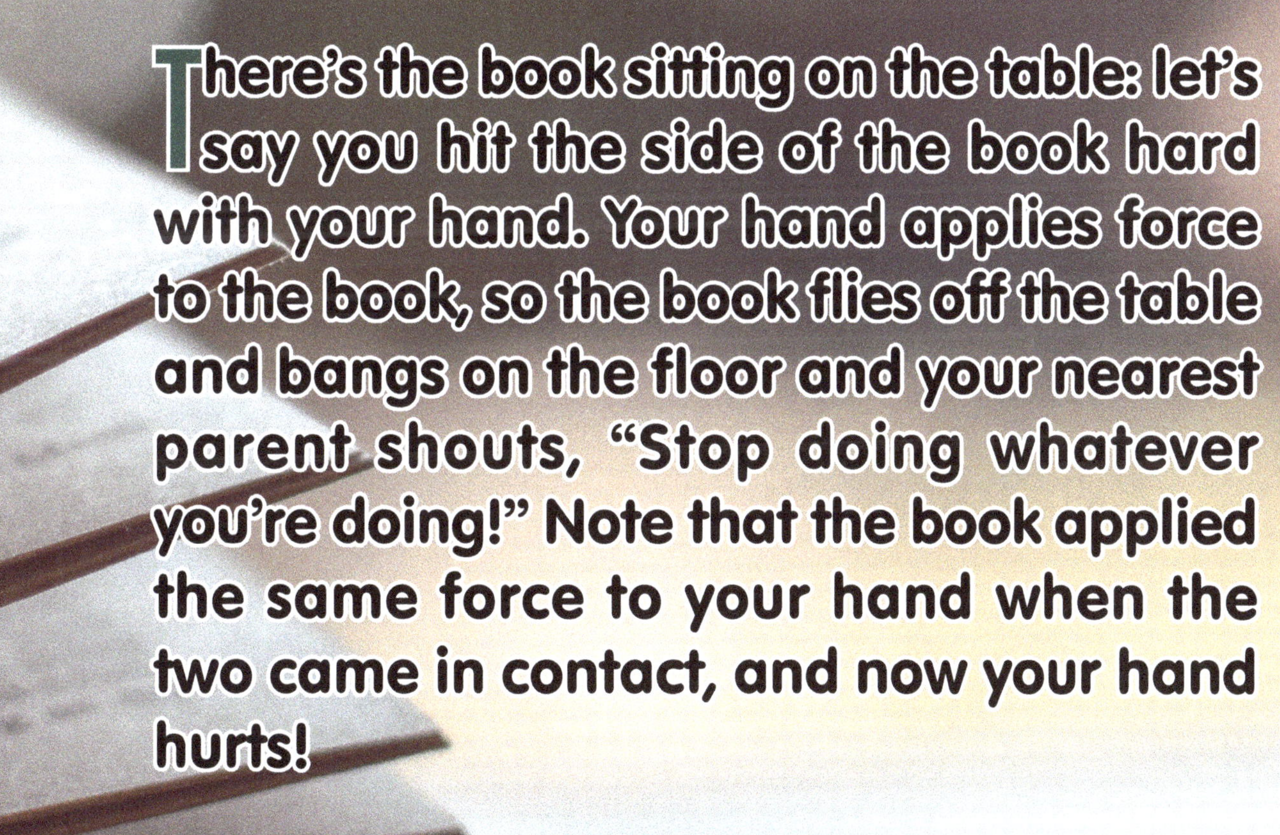

There's the book sitting on the table: let's say you hit the side of the book hard with your hand. Your hand applies force to the book, so the book flies off the table and bangs on the floor and your nearest parent shouts, "Stop doing whatever you're doing!" Note that the book applied the same force to your hand when the two came in contact, and now your hand hurts!

FRICTIONAL FORCE

Friction happens when two object slide along each other: they generate frictional force.

The photo on the right page shows frictional force. A sound is created because of the friction between the string and the bow.

If you have a frozen surface, like a hockey rink, and you slide an ice cube along the surface, the ice cube will slide quite a long way because there is little frictional force to slow it down. But if you try to slide the same ice cube, with the same initial energy, over a pebbly beach, the ice cube won't get far. The friction between the ice cube and the pebbles will be much higher.

When you apply the brakes on your bike to slow down, you are using frictional force, and it's a good thing. But frictional force can be a bad thing: if pieces of an engine start rubbing on each other when they aren't supposed to, they can create a frictional force that causes both pieces of metal to heat up and maybe break, melt, or just stop working. That would be a bad result!

PLAYING TUG OF WAR

TENSION FORCE

Tension force happens when you pull something to its fullest extension. Let's say you have a rope tied to a tree, and you take the other end of the rope and you and five friends pull on that end until the rope is as straight as it can go. You have created a tension force that affects the rope, the tree, and all five of you pulling on it!

SPRING FORCE

Not surprisingly a spring force is related to a spring. When you compress a spring it stores up potential energy in each coil of the spring. When you release the spring, coil by coil the spring releases its potential energy to expand to its uncompressed (and unstretched) state.

WE BOUNCE WHEN WE JUMP ON THE TRAMPOLINE. THIS IS BECAUSE OF THE SPRING FORCE APPLIED FROM THE SPRINGS.

THERE WILL BE AIR
RESISTANCE ONCE THE
PARACHUTE IS OPENED.

RESISTANCE FORCE

Resistance force happens when one object puts pressure on another object, and the second object responds.

The photo on the left page shows that there is a Resistance Force involved.

Watch a leaf blowing down the road. If the wind is light, the leaf can create enough resistance force to make the wind go around it while the leaf stays still. If the

wind is stronger, it overcomes the leaf's resistance force and the leaf goes tumbling down the street.

YOU APPLY FORCE WHENEVER YOU OPEN AND CLOSE A DOOR.

OBJECTS AT A DISTANCE

Some forces can be created even when objects are not in direct contact with each other. They can still create a push or a pull.

GRAVITATIONAL FORCE

Every object that has mass creates a gravitational force that pulls on other objects with mass, even when they are far away from each other. For example, the Earth is moving very fast through space, but the gravitational force of the Sun keeps pulling the Earth so its path is not a straight line, but an orbit around the Sun.

WE WILL JUST FLOAT IN THE AIR
IF THERE'S NO GRAVITY

As another example, our Moon is about 239,000 miles from the Earth, but it exerts a gravitational force that causes the water in Earth's oceans to rise and fall twice a day, creating what we call "tides". Read the Baby Professor book *Can I Dance on the Moon?* To learn more about gravity.

ELECTRIC FORCE

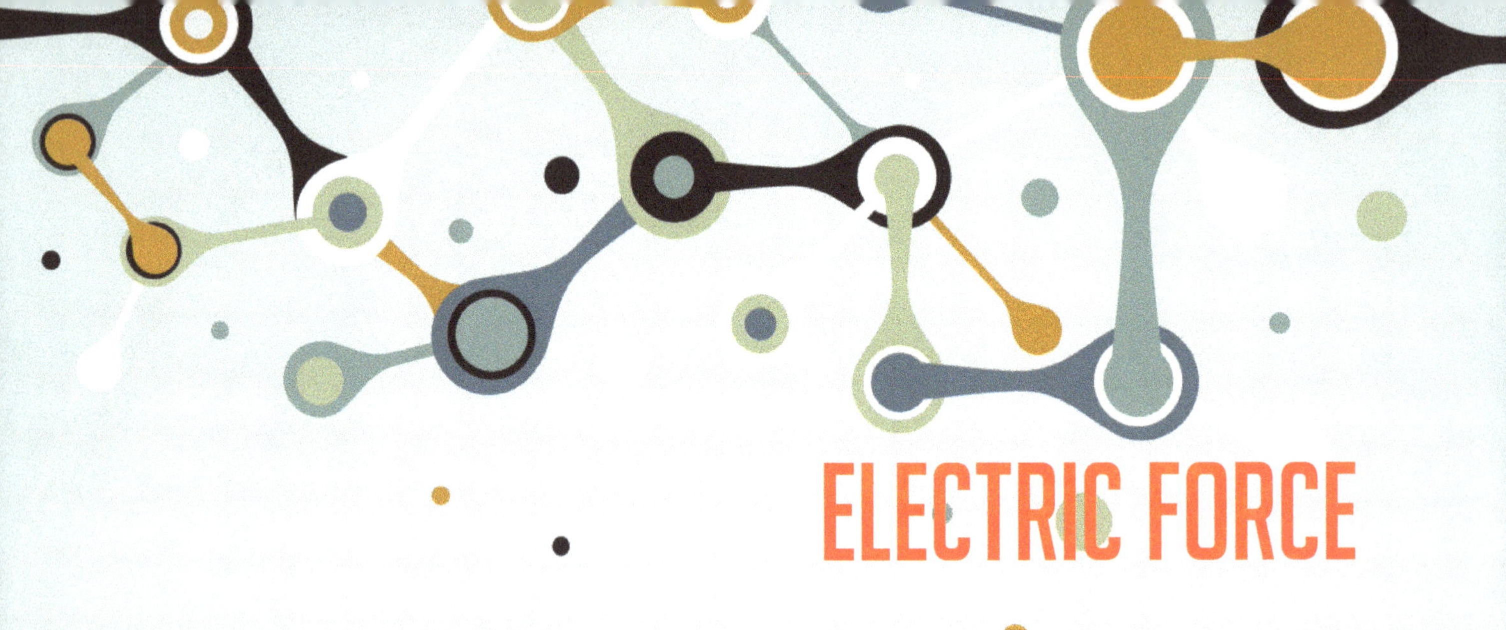

A force that acts at a distance, even though the distances are tiny, is electric force. This force operates at the atomic level. The nucleus of an atom and its electrons are not actually touching, but they still create an electric force that pulls the nucleus and the electrons toward each other.

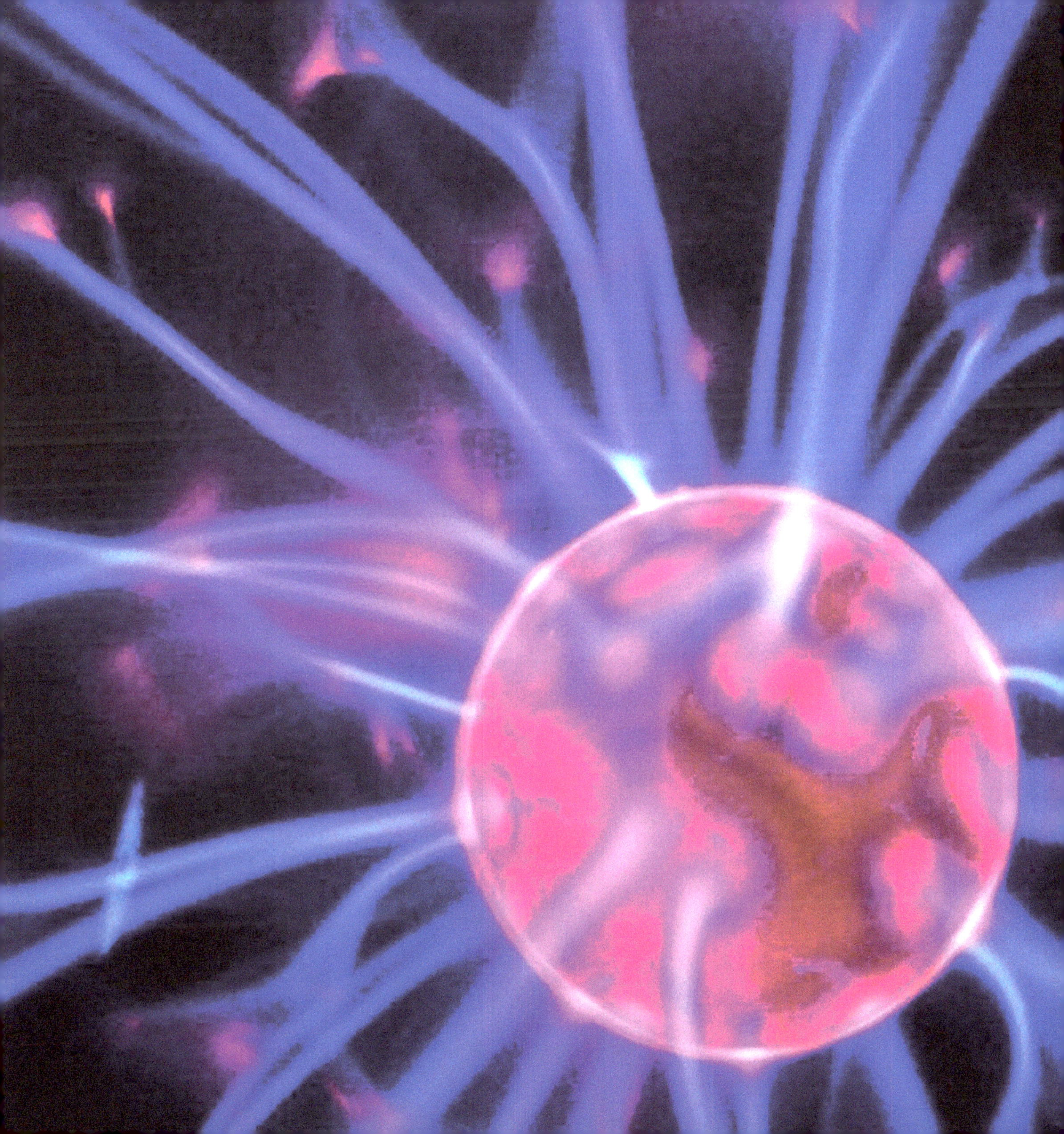

AS321238CB
A4

MAGNETIC FORCE

If you have a magnet and some pins that you dropped on the floor and you want to pick them up before your nearest parent notices the mess, you can use the magnet to exert a magnetic force on the pins. If you hold the magnet near to the pins, they will rise up to the magnet, responding to the pull of its magnetic force.

Magnets have positive and negative poles, or ends. If you put two positives or two negatives close to each other, they will create a magnetic force that pushes the two magnets apart. If you put a positive and a negative end close to each other, they will create a magnetic force that draws the two magnets toward each other.

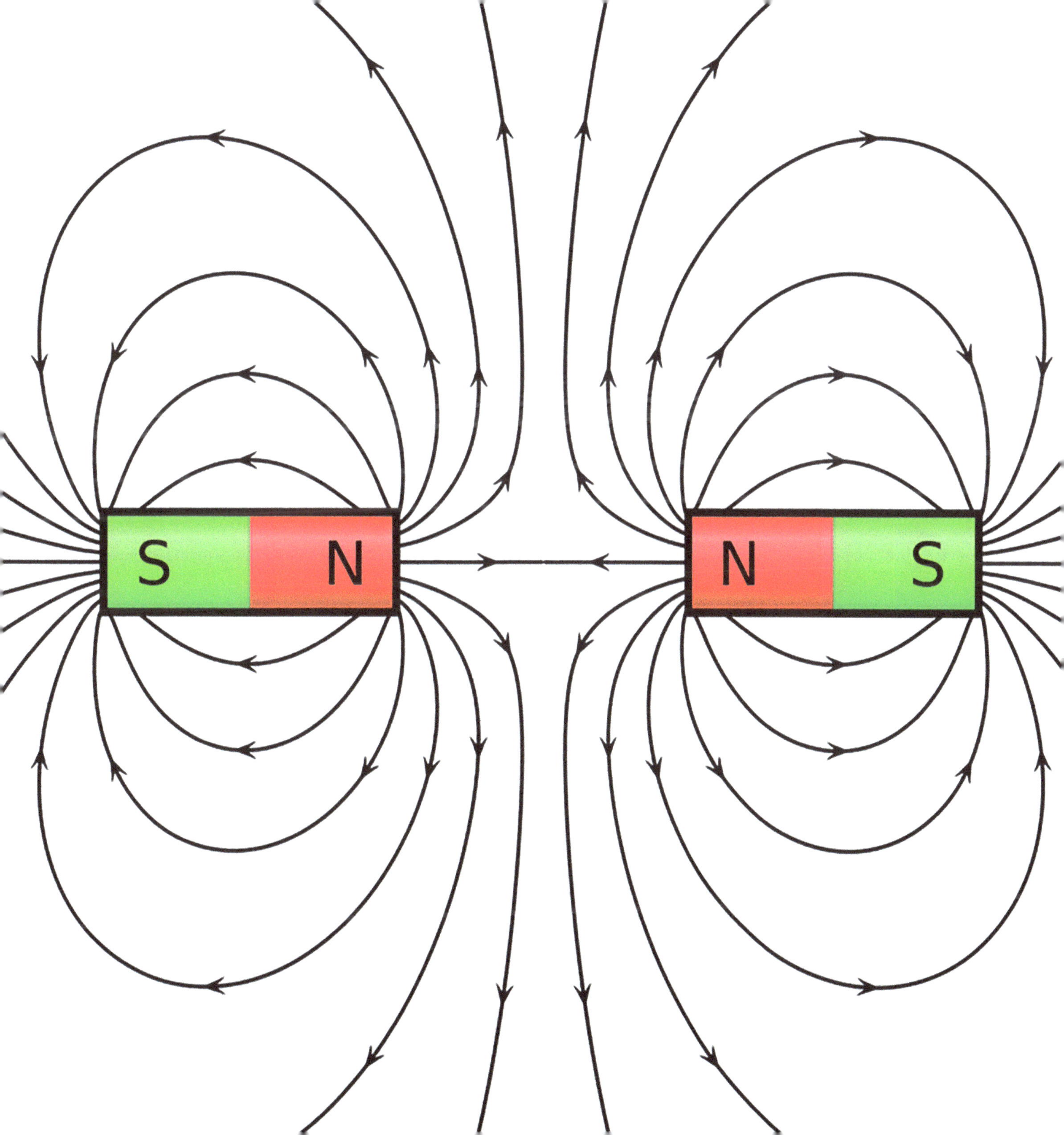

S
N
N
S

THIS BOY IS USING FORCE BY PUSHING THE BALL BY USING HIS LEG.

FORCE IS A VECTOR

In physics, a force is a "vector". This means a force has both magnitude (how strong it is) and a direction (where it is pulling from or pushing toward). When you describe the force acting between two objects, you have to provide both the magnitude and the direction.

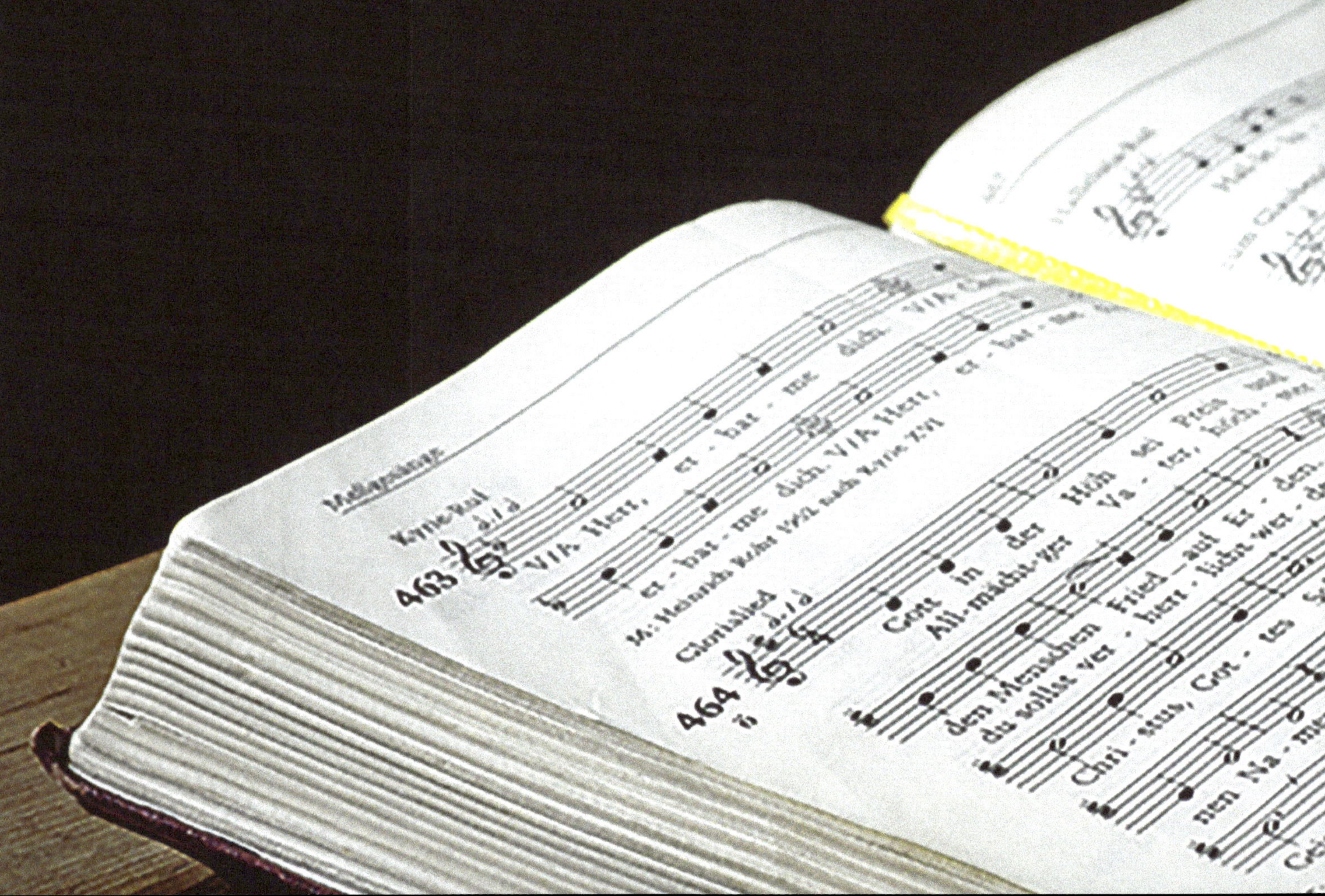

Remember the book on the table that you hit with your hand? If you hit it with your hand travelling left to right, the book will fly off the table and hit the floor to your right. If your hand travels right to left, the book will go somewhere else.

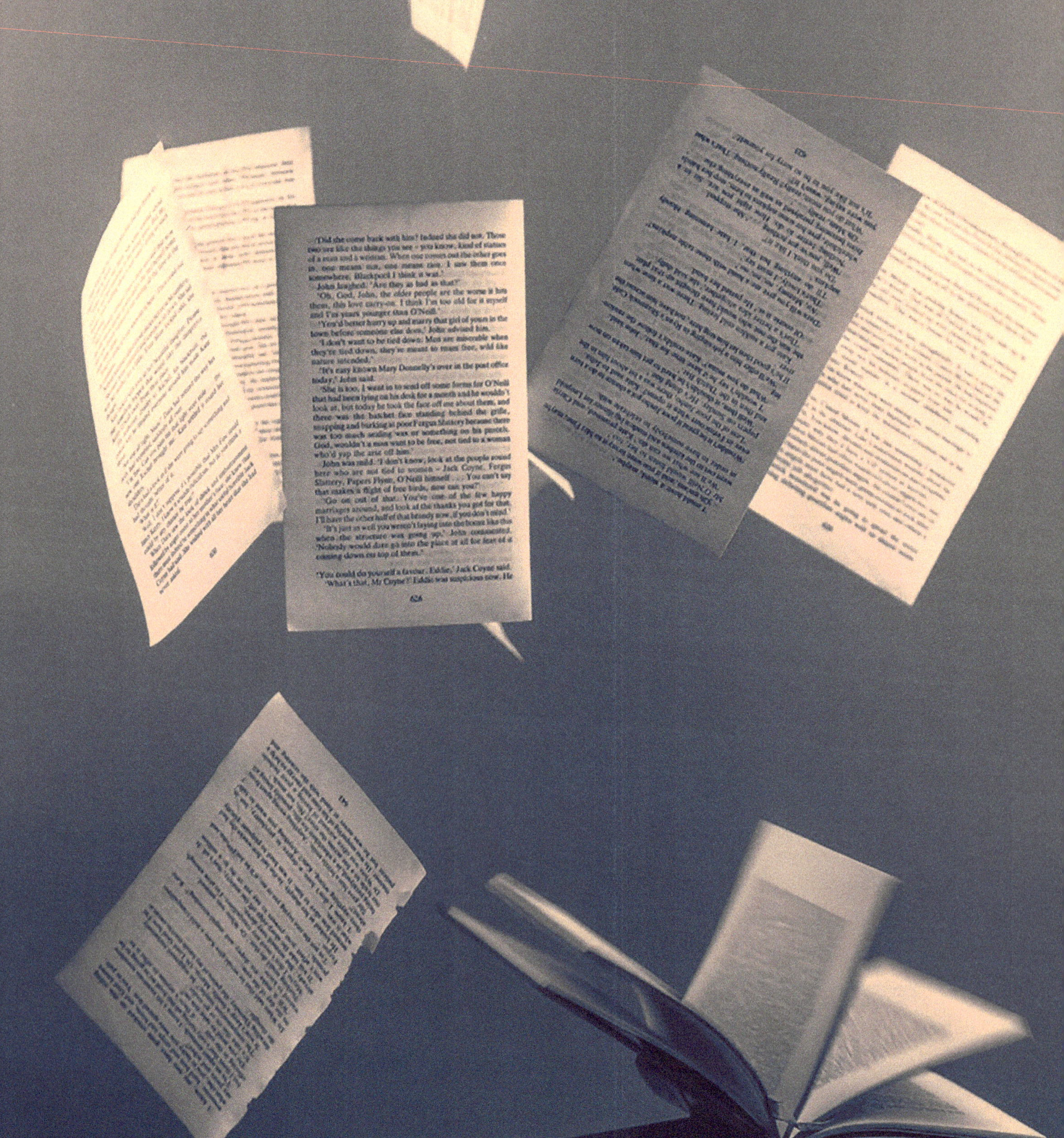
'Did she come back with him? Indeed she did not. These two are like the things you see – you know, kind of statues of a man and a woman. When one comes out the other goes in, one means sun, one means rain. I saw them once somewhere, Blackpool I think it was.'
John laughed. 'Are they as bad as that?'
'Oh, God, John, the older people are the worse it hits them, this love carry-on. I think I'm too old for it myself and I'm years younger than O'Neill.'
'You'd better hurry up and marry that girl of yours in the town before someone else does,' John advised him.
'I don't want to be tied down. Men are miserable when they're tied down, they're meant to roam free, wild like nature intended.'
'It's easy known Mary Donnelly's over at the post office today,' John said.
'She is too. I went in to send off some forms for O'Neill that had been lying on his desk for a month and he wouldn't look at, but today he took the face off me about them, and there was the basket face standing behind the grille, snapping and barking at poor Fergus Slattery because there was too much sealing wax or something on his parcels. God, wouldn't a man want to be free, not tied to a woman who'd yap the arse off him.'
John was mild. 'I don't know, look at the people round here who are not tied to women – Jack Coyne, Fergus Slattery, Papers Flynn, O'Neill himself . . . You can't say that makes a flight of free birds, now can you?'
'Go on, out of that. You're one of the few happy marriages around, and look at the thanks you got for that. I'll have the other half of that brandy now, if you don't mind.'
'It's just as well you weren't laying into the booze like this when the structure was going up,' John commented. 'Nobody would dare go into the place at all for fear of it coming down on top of them.'

'You could do yourself a favour, Eddie,' Jack Coyne said.
'What's that, Mr Coyne?' Eddie was suspicious now. He

And if you hit the book with your hand going straight down, the book may not move at all if the table is sturdy enough that it can provide an upward force equal to your hand's downward force. Your hand will still hurt because of the upward force the table and the book applied to you, but the book is probably still on the table.

PUSHING AND PULLING

In physics, most forces are pushes and pulls. When you rub your hands together, the friction force (a push force) both slows your hands down and warms them up. Gravity is working on you all the time: it's a pull force that keeps you from floating out your window and up into the air!

PUSHING AND PULLING IS APPLIED WHEN SLICING

A push force moves one of the objects involved in the direction of the push, and the other object in the opposite direction. When you push someone on a swing, you give a push force to that person, and you also receive a push force away from the swing from that person. That's why you have to plant your feet and lean forward when you push.

When several forces push and pull at the same time on an object, they can make the force larger on the object or cancel it out. Let's say you're dribbling a basketball. The ball will fall by itself when you let it go because of the pull force of gravity. But when you dribble you add a downward push force with your hand to make the ball go down faster and hit the ground harder. This causes the ground to cause a push force on the ball to send it back up to your hand again.

ISAAC NEWTON

THREE BASIC LAWS

Sir Isaac Newton was an English scientist who studied force. He developed three important laws related to force and motion:

A body that is in motion will probably stay in motion, and a body at rest will probably stay at rest, unless some force acts on it.

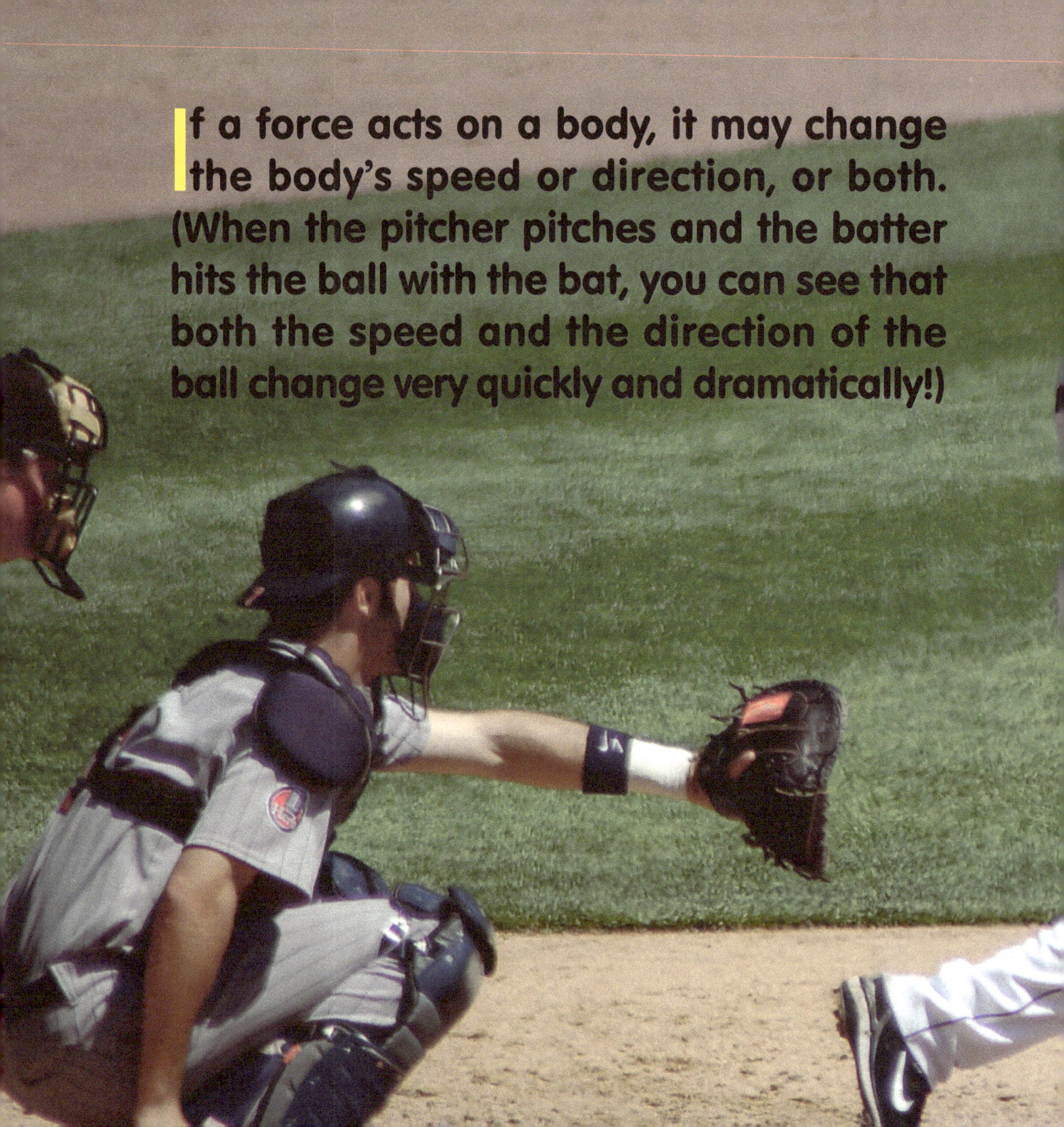

If a force acts on a body, it may change the body's speed or direction, or both. (When the pitcher pitches and the batter hits the ball with the bat, you can see that both the speed and the direction of the ball change very quickly and dramatically!)

APPLIED FORCE WHEN PLAYING BASEBALL

APPLIED FORCE WHEN PLAYING SOCCER

For every action, there is an equal and opposite reaction. When you knock the book off the table you exert force on the book, and the book exerts force on your hand.

SCIENCE GOVERNS THE WORLD

The rules of science make the world act the way it does. Read Baby Professor books like Speed, Velocity, and Acceleration to learn even more about the rules of science.

Visit
BABY PROFESSOR
EDUCATION KIDS
www.BabyProfessorBooks.com
to download Free Baby Professor eBooks and view
our catalog of new and exciting Children's Books

* 9 7 9 8 8 6 9 4 1 1 8 8 4 *